Collage

Sue Nicholson

QEB Publishing

Copyright © QEB Publishing, Inc. 2005

Published in the United States by
QEB Publishing, Inc.
23062 La Cadena Drive
Laguna Hills, CA 92653

www.qeb-publishing.com

Library of Congress Control Number: 2005921166

ISBN 1-59566-082-8

Written by Sue Nicholson
Designed by Susi Martin
Editor Paul Manning

Publisher Steve Evans
Creative Director Louise Morley
Editorial Manager Jean Coppendale

The author and publisher would like to thank:
Sam, Georgina and Christopher
Sarah Morley for making the models
Evie Fitzpatrick for the full body collage on page 13

Printed and bound in China

Note to teachers and parents

The projects in this book are aimed at children in
grades 1–3 and are presented in order of difficulty,
from easy to more challenging. Each can be used as a
stand-alone activity or as part of another area of study.

While the ideas in the book are offered as inspiration,
children should always be encouraged to work from
their own imagination and first-hand observations.

All projects in this book require adult supervision.

Sourcing ideas

★ Encourage the children to source ideas from their
   own experiences as well as from magazines,
   books, the Internet, art galleries, or museums.
★ Prompt them to talk about different types of art
   they have seen at home or on vacation.
★ Use the "Click for Art!" boxes as a starting point
   for finding useful material on the Internet.*

★ Suggest that each child keeps a sketchbook
   of their ideas.

Evaluating work

★ Encourage the children to share their work and talk
   about their ideas and ways of working. What do
   they like best/least about it? If they did it again,
   what would they do differently?
★ Help the children judge the originality of their work
   and appreciate the different qualities in others'
   work. This will help them value ways of working
   that are different from their own
★ Encourage the children by displaying their work.

* Website information is correct at the time of going to
   press. However, the publishers cannot accept liability
   for information or links found on third-party websites.

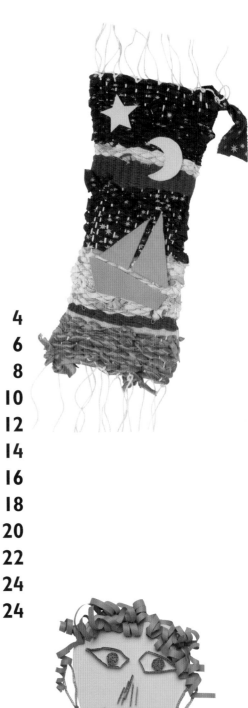

Contents

Words in bold, **like this**, are explained in the Glossary on page 24.

Getting started

A collage is a picture made from scraps of paper or other materials. You can use anything in a collage, from cardboard and string to sequins—but ask first!

Here are some things you will need:

Top tip
Don't forget to spread out some newspaper to work on, and wear an apron or old shirt to keep your clothes clean.

Paper
You can use all kinds of paper in your collages. Collect:

- Newspaper and magazines
- Shiny card stock and posterboard
- Tissue paper and tracing paper
- Crêpe paper, brown paper, and construction paper
- Wallpaper and sandpaper
- Lacy doilies, used stamps, and candy wrappers

Safety scissors

Basic equipment

- Paper and cardboard
- Poster/**acrylic** paints
- Pencils and paintbrushes
- Scissors and ruler
- **White glue** and masking tape

You will also need some extra items, which are listed separately for each project.

Collage box

Keep a box to collect objects and materials with an interesting **texture** or shape—like buttons, beads, yarn, string, or bubble wrap. See the list on page 14 for more ideas.

For your mount board

- Piece of cardboard or posterboard
- Sides cut from a cardboard box

Glue

Masking and sticky tape

Get weaving!

You can **weave** your own cloth to use in your collages. Turn to page 20 to find out how it's done.

Be careful!

Collage projects often involve cutting, gluing, and spraying. When cutting, always use safety scissors, and ask an adult to help you where you see this sign:

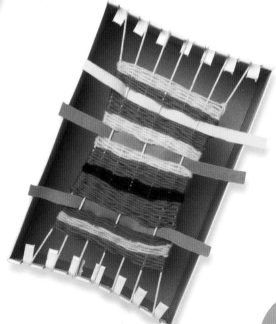

"Me" collage

Tell a story about yourself through a collage. The **theme** could be a birthday, a favorite hobby, a vacation—or what about your favorite things?

Soccer collage ideas

A soccer collage could include:

★ Team photos
★ Scraps from a soccer program
★ Ticket stubs from a match
★ Newspaper headlines about soccer stars
★ Fabric from an old soccer shirt
★ Shoelaces or cleats

You will need:

- Materials for your collage
- Cardboard or posterboard

1 Collect lots of things that tell a story. If you're not sure what to do, look at the red and blue boxes on these pages for ideas.

Top tip

Always ask an adult for help with cutting and gluing.

3 Glue down all the things to your piece of **mount board** with white glue. Glue a small area at a time.

2 Arrange all the things you have collected on a cardboard mount board. Move them around until you are happy with the way they look.

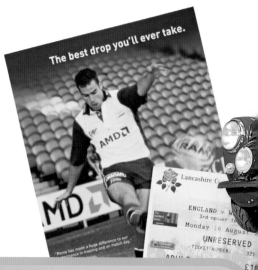

The best drop you'll ever take.

Click for Art!

To see a photocollage by David Hockney, go to **http://artlex.com/** and search for "Photocollage."

6

Fun collage made from ticket stubs, postcards, and other vacation souvenirs

Vacation collage ideas

★ Photographs from travel brochures or magazines

★ Ticket stubs and luggage tags

★ A sprinkling of sand and shells

★ Food and candy wrappers

★ Postcards and stamps

★ Foreign coins

Magazine collage

Make a collage from scraps cut or torn from magazines. Choose a theme you find interesting—this one is about food. Look at the collage themes box for other ideas.

Collage themes

- ★ Animals
- ★ Ballet
- ★ Cars
- ★ Colors
- ★ Dinosaurs
- ★ Dogs
- ★ Faces
- ★ Flowers
- ★ Sports
- ★ Happiness
- ★ Horse-riding
- ★ Robots
- ★ Space
- ★ Winter

You will need:

- Plenty of old newspapers and magazines
- Cardboard or posterboard

1 Find pictures in magazines about your theme. Using safety scissors, cut out as many pictures as you can.

2 Arrange the pictures on your mount board until you like the way they look.

3 Glue the pictures onto the mount board.

Click for Art! To see a collage by Picasso, go to **www.tate.org.uk** click on "Collection," then search on "Picasso" and "Bottle of Vieux Marc, Glass, Guitar, and Newspaper."

3D pictures

To make a picture stand out from the cardboard mount:

1 Glue the picture onto lightweight cardboard. Cut out around the picture.

2 Fold a strip of cardboard in half, then in half again. Open it out a little, so it looks like a chair with the bottom folded under.

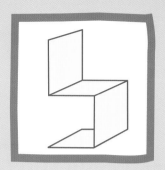

3 Glue the flat part at the top to the mount board.

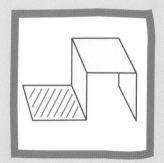

4 Glue the picture to the raised part that sticks out at the front.

Food collage using pictures cut from magazines

Paper collage

You can use all kinds of paper in a collage. Collect plain colored paper, construction paper, wrapping paper, wallpaper, candy wrappers, tissue paper, and newspaper.

Paper parrot

You will need:
- Different colors and textures of paper for the collage
- Cardboard or posterboard

Top tip
Try using layers of colored tissue papers so the top color mixes with the color below.

This parrot has been made from different kinds of paper, cut into shapes, and then glued in place.

1 First plan your picture. Draw the picture lightly with a pencil on the mount board.

Click for Art!
To see a collage by Matisse, go to **www.tate.org.uk** click on "Collection," then search "Matisse/The Snail."

2 Using safety scissors, cut out the different kinds of paper into the shapes you want for each part of the picture.

3 Move the pieces of paper around on your drawing until they look right.

4 Glue down the paper shapes, one at a time. To overlap shapes, glue larger pieces first, then smaller ones on top.

Fish shapes cut from foil

Tissue paper strips for seaweed

Sandy ocean floor cut from sandpaper

Collage face

The collage face on page 13 was made from cardboard that was cut, folded, and rolled in different ways.

The collage face on page 13

There are lots of ways to make cardboard into different shapes.

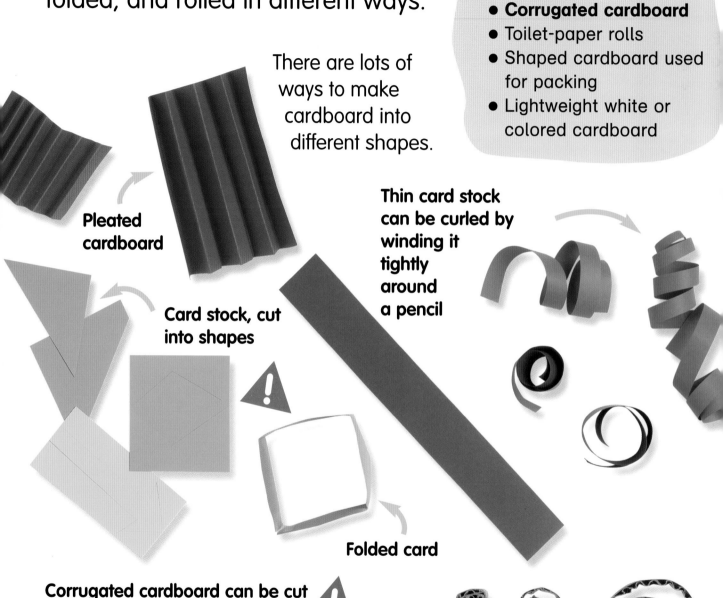

Cardboard crazy!

How many types of cardboard can you find?
Try collecting:

- Empty food boxes
- Card stock
- **Corrugated cardboard**
- Toilet-paper rolls
- Shaped cardboard used for packing
- Lightweight white or colored cardboard

Pleated cardboard

Thin card stock can be curled by winding it tightly around a pencil

Card stock, cut into shapes

Folded card

Corrugated cardboard can be cut into a shape and stuck down flat...

... or cut into a long strip and rolled into a tight circle ...

... or a loose spiral that sticks up from the mount board

Life-size body collage

Ask a friend to lie down on a long piece of paper and draw around him or her with a pencil. Lightly draw in the face. Glue down lots of different materials such as yarn, fabric, felt, torn paper, sequins, or ribbons to make the face and clothes.

Hair made of thin, green card stock, rolled into spirals

Eyes made out of tightly rolled corrugated cardboard

Cardboard glued in wavy lines to make the mouth

Earrings made from pleated card stock

Scrap collage

It's fun to mix different materials and objects in a collage. Here's how to make a picture from scrap materials you may find around your home.

You will need:
- Cardboard or posterboard for mounting
- Objects and materials for the collage (see below)
- Gold or silver spray paint

Paper clips

Foil

Fabric background

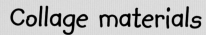

Street scene made from scrap materials

Collage materials

Look out for these scrap materials to use in your collage:

- Buttons and shells
- String, yarn, and rubber bands
- Scraps of cardboard
- Fabric, ribbon, and thread
- Washers, nuts, bolts, nails, or screws
- Sponges and corks
- Twigs, feathers, and leaves
- Foil and bottle tops
- Bubble wrap, cellophane, and styrofoam

1 Draw the outline of a car on the mount board with a pencil.

Junk car

Screws

This car was made from scrap materials glued to corrugated cardboard. It was then spray-painted silver.

Small coins and bottletop wheels

2 Using safety scissors, cut shapes out of paper, cardboard, or plastic to fit parts of the car, or arrange items such as buttons, nails, or washers in rows.

3 Keep arranging and rearranging the shapes until you are happy with the way they look.

4 Glue down your collage, one small area at a time.

Click for Art!

To see a collage using scrap plastic and other materials, go to **www.tate.org.uk** click on "Collection" then search on "Tony Cragg" and "Britain Seen from the North."

Food collage

Use dried foods, glued to a strong cardboard mount board, to make an imaginative food collage!

You will need:

- Dried food (see box)
- Black paper
- Cardboard for the mount
- White or yellow pencil
- Tweezers

1 Glue the black paper onto a strong piece of cardboard as a mount board.

Food collage ideas

Food collages work best if you choose a simple pattern or picture. For example:

★ a flower
★ a tiger
★ a lizard
★ a snake with a zigzag pattern on its back

2 Plan your picture on a piece of white paper first. When you are happy with it, draw it onto the black paper with a white or yellow pencil.

3 Choose dried foods for the different parts of your picture. Sprinkle a few beans, lentils, or seeds in each area to remind you what goes where.

Top tip

Ask an adult to spray the finished collage with glue or shellac to keep the dried food in place.

Food collage with border made from pasta wheels

5 Leave the collage flat until the glue has dried completely.

4 Spread glue thickly over a small part of the picture. Sprinkle small seeds over the glue. You can use tweezers to position larger items.

Dried foods

- Red and green lentils
- Dried beans and peas
- Pasta shapes and spaghetti
- Black, white, and brown rice
- Sunflower and poppy seeds
- Pine nuts

Fabric collage

Collages made out of different fabrics are great to look at—and to touch!

Clouds made from scraps of netting and lace

Sheep's soft coats made from wool

You will need:

- Scraps of fabric
- Wide-eye needle and thread (optional) **!**
- Thick cloth or cardboard for the mount

Collecting fabrics

Look out for fabrics with different textures, such as scratchy burlap, smooth silk, and soft furs. Buy left over pieces from stores or junk sales, or cut up old clothes—but always check with an adult first! **!**

1 Plan your picture and draw it lightly onto the mount.

2 Using safety scissors, cut the fabric into shapes.

Click for Art!

To see fabrics used in a collage, go to
www.makleindesign.com/AdvancedFabricCollageideas.htm

Flowers made from scrunched-up scraps of brightly colored fabric

Top tip

If you don't want edges of cloth to fray, cut your fabric with pinking shears to give a zigzag edge.

Working with fabrics

You can use fabrics in a similar way to paper:

- Pleating: Glue the fabric down as you pleat it, or tack it with big rough stitches using a needle and thread.
- Scrunching: Crumple the fabric and glue it down.
- Twisting: Twist the fabric, then glue it in place.
- Braiding: Braid strands of different fabrics into one.
- Cutting: Cut fabric into shapes to stick onto another material, or cut holes so you can see through to the fabric below.

3 Arrange the shapes on the mount until you are happy with the way they look. See the pink box for ways of giving your collage an interesting 3-D effect.

4 Glue down the shapes, one small area at a time.

Straw weaving

Woven cloth is good to use in a collage especially if you weave it yourself!
To get started, here's how to make a woven wall-hanging using yarn and plastic straws.

You will need:
- Plastic straws
- Cardboard
- Yarn, string, or embroidery thread for weaving

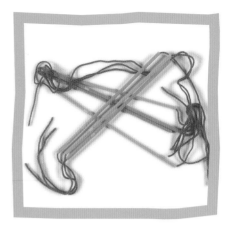

I Take some plastic straws and thread a length of yarn through each one. The yarn should be 8 in (20 cm) longer than the straws.

Add a second color to make stripes

Push this straw down to tighten the threads

Top tip
Try wrapping the yarn around a strip of cardboard—this makes it easier to push the threads in and out.

4 Weave a straw at the top and bottom to hold your yarn in place. Your decoration is now ready to hang on the wall.

2 Knot the ends of the yarn loosely together at the top and bottom. Then tape the knots to a sheet of cardboard. Make sure the straws are flat.

3 Weave yarn in and out of the straws from left to right, then right to left. If you like, make some stripes using different-colored yarn.

Making a simple loom

Here's how to set up a simple cardboard **loom** for the weaving project on page 22.

You will need:

- A shoebox
- Yarn or string for weaving

1 Ask an adult to help you make a series of notches ½ in (1.5 cm) deep and ½ in (1.5 cm) apart in the sides of a shoebox.

2 Tape the end of a long piece of yarn or string to one side of the box. Wrap the yarn or string around and around the box, using the notches to hold it in place. These are your **warp** threads.

3 Cut the end of the yarn and tape it to the side of the box.

Now turn to page 22 to get weaving!

21

Woven fabric collage

Use the simple cardboard loom on page 21 to weave fun fabrics for your pictures and collages.

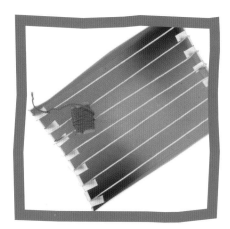  

1 Wind a long piece of yarn around a strip of cardboard that you can easily hold in your fingers. Tie the loose end of the yarn around the first warp thread on your loom.

2 Using the card, weave the yarn under and over each of the warp threads to form the **weft**.

3 At the end of each row, pull the weft threads down toward you, using your fingers.

Top tip
Wind a long thread firmly around each warp thread at the top and bottom of the loom. This gives a neat, strong edge to your woven cloth.

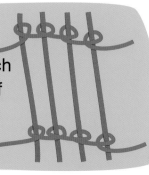

Click for Art!

To see examples of beautiful woven carpets, go to **http://weavingartmuseum.org/main.html**

4 Keep weaving until you have covered all the long warp threads. Knot the loose end of the weft thread.

5 Cut the warp threads on the bottom of the box. Knot the threads together. Cut off the extra string or leave it as a fringe.

Fabric collage

Use woven cloth as the background for a fabric collage.

1 Weave strips of fabric and yarn between your warp threads to make bands of different colors and textures.

2 Cut out shapes from felt, such as a moon, star, and a boat.

3 Glue the fabric shapes onto your **tapestry** with fabric glue, or ask an adult to help you sew them on.

Glossary

acrylic   easy-to-mix paint that can be cleaned with soap and water

corrugated   type of cardboard shaped into folds with a pattern of ridges and grooves

loom   device used to weave fibers (such as yarn or cotton thread) together to make cloth or fabric

mount board   piece of cardboard or paper on which things are stuck down

tapestry   cloth that has been woven on a frame

texture   the surface or "feel" of something—for example, rough, soft, smooth, or furry

theme   the subject of something, such as an idea for a story

warp   threads strung across a loom

weave   to make cloth by passing threads or strands under and over each other

weft   threads crossing over and under the warp threads on a loom

white glue   strong craft glue that does not wash away

Index